Girls For The Win!

Girls on the VOLLEYBALL TEAM

Beth Gottlieb

Enslow PUBLISHING

DISCOVER!

Please visit our website, www.enslow.com. For a free color catalog of all our high-quality books, call toll free 1-800-398-2504 or fax 1-877-980-4454.

Library of Congress Cataloging-in-Publication Data
Names: Gottlieb, Beth, author.
Title: Girls on the volleyball team / Beth Gottlieb.
Description: New York, N.Y. : Enslow Publishing, [2023] | Series: Girls for the win! | Includes bibliographical references and index.
Identifiers: LCCN 2021046436 (print) | LCCN 2021046437 (ebook) | ISBN 9781978528246 (library binding) | ISBN 9781978528222 (paperback) | ISBN 9781978528239 (set) | ISBN 9781978528253 (ebook)
Subjects: LCSH: Volleyball–Juvenile literature. | Volleyball for women–Juvenile literature.
Classification: LCC GV1015.34 .G67 2023 (print) | LCC GV1015.34 (ebook) | DDC 796.325082–dc23/eng/20211020
LC record available at https://lccn.loc.gov/2021046436
LC ebook record available at https://lccn.loc.gov/2021046437

Published in 2023 by
Enslow Publishing
29 E. 21st Street
New York, NY 10010

Designer: Katelyn E. Reynolds
Interior Design: Tanya Dellaccio
Editor: Kristen Nelson

Photo credits: Cover (girl) supparsorn/Shutterstock.com; cover (series art) LHF Graphics/Shutterstock.com; p. 5 NoSystem images/iStockphoto.com; p. 7 (inset) https://upload.wikimedia.org/wikipedia/commons/c/cc/Women_playing_volleyball_at_the_University_of_Washington%2C_ca_1923_%28MOHAI_5492%29.jpg; p. 7 (main) https://upload.wikimedia.org/wikipedia/commons/8/86/1978PittVBallteam.jpg; p. 9 miodrag ignjatovic/iStockphoto.com; pp. 10, 14 DnDavis/Shutterstock.com; p. 11 Chris Radburn/AP Images; p. 13 muzsy/Shutterstock.com; p. 15 Stuart Monk/Shutterstock.com; p. 17 dotshock/Shutterstock.com; p. 19 Yucel Cakiroglu/Shutterstock.com; p. 21 A.RICARDO/Shutterstock.com.

Portions of this work were originally authored by Anne Forest and published as *Girls Play Volleyball*. All new material this edition authored by Beth Gottlieb.

Printed in the United States of America

CPSIA compliance information: Batch #CSENS23: For further information contact Enslow Publishing, New York, New York, at 1-800-398-2504.

CONTENTS

Get on the Team! 4
Volleyball's Start 6
On the Court 8
Game Time 12
Volleyball Pros 18
Olympic Dreams 20
Words to Know 22
For More Information 23
Index 24

Boldface words appear in Words to Know.

GET ON THE TEAM!

Volleyball is a sport that needs a lot of teamwork. No one player can win a game for her team. Volleyball players need to think and move quickly. Are you ready to join the team?

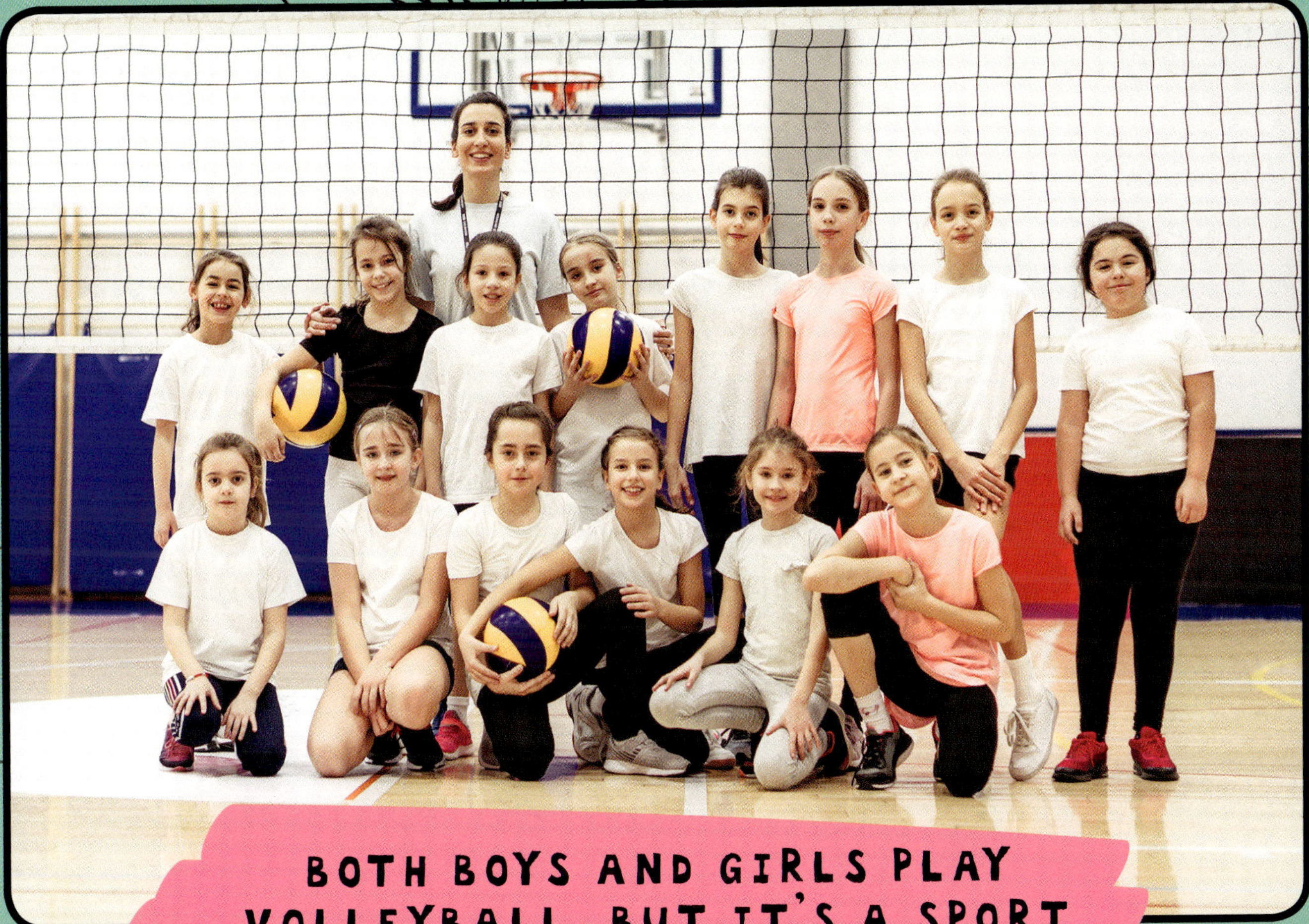

BOTH BOYS AND GIRLS PLAY VOLLEYBALL. BUT IT'S A SPORT THAT'S GROWING AMONG GIRLS AND WOMEN ALL OVER THE WORLD.

VOLLEYBALL'S START

Volleyball's history starts with basketball! Some men found basketball to be too hard on their body. With that in mind, William G. Morgan invented a sport that had players hit a ball over a net in 1895. By the mid-1900s, both men and women played volleyball.

THE FIRST WORLD **CHAMPIONSHIP** FOR WOMEN'S VOLLEYBALL WAS HELD IN 1952.

ON THE COURT

There are two main kinds of volleyball. Indoor volleyball is played on an indoor court. Outdoor volleyball—also called beach volleyball—is played outside on sand. Many schools have indoor volleyball teams. Players can start learning as young children!

GIRLS ARE PLAYING INDOOR VOLLEYBALL ON TEAMS ALL OVER THE WORLD!

Indoor volleyball is played with teams of six. Three players stand in the front row, and three players stand in the back row on one side of a net. They work to score more points than the other team.

VOLLEYBALL GAMES, OR MATCHES, HAVE PARTS CALLED SETS.

GAME TIME

A player **serves** the ball over the net to the other team's side of the court. The other team tries to hit the ball back over the net. A team gets a point if the ball touches the other team's side of the court.

A TEAM ALSO CAN SCORE A POINT IF THE OTHER TEAM **COMMITS** A **FAULT**.

A player keeps serving the ball until her team commits a fault or the other team gets the ball to hit the floor on her side of the court. When that happens, the other team gets a chance to serve.

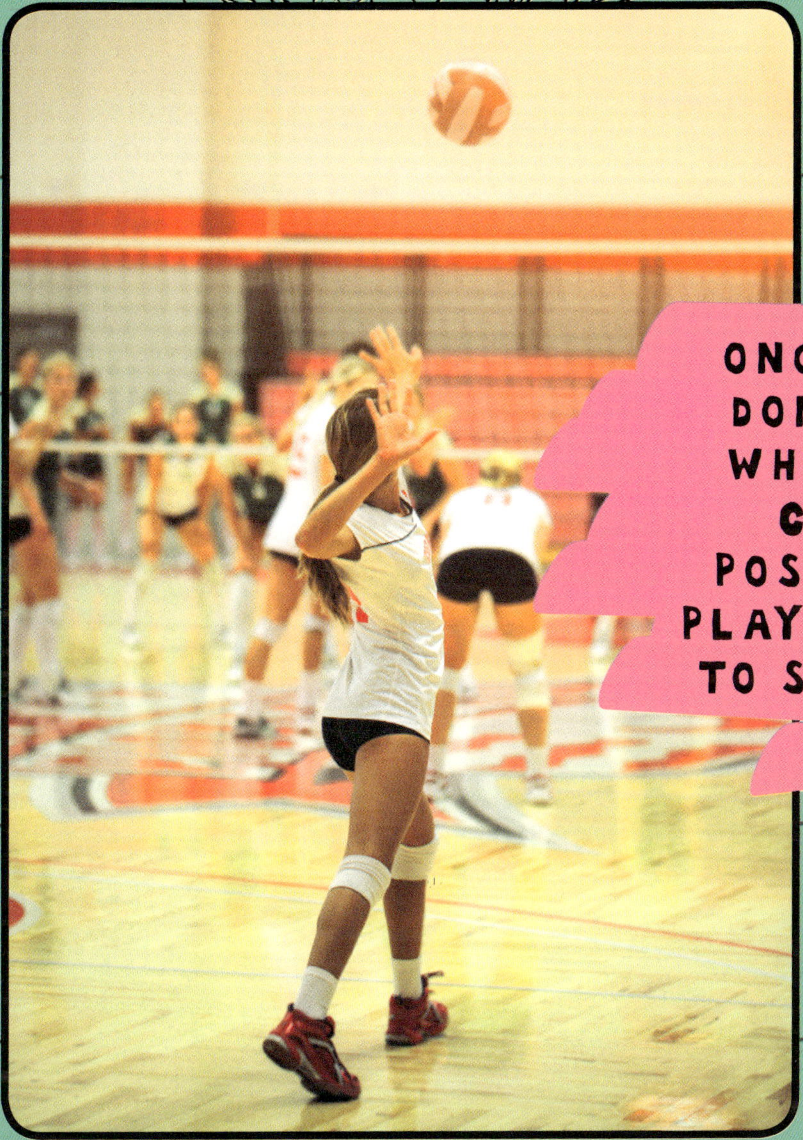

ONCE ONE PLAYER IS DONE SERVING, THE WHOLE TEAM MOVES **CLOCKWISE** ONE POSITION, SO A NEW PLAYER GETS A CHANCE TO SERVE NEXT TIME.

The first team to score 25 points wins a set in indoor volleyball. However, in order to win a set, a team must win by at least two points. The first team to win three sets wins the whole match.

IF A MATCH HAS TO GO TO FIVE SETS, THE WINNER OF THE FIFTH SET ONLY NEEDS TO SCORE 15 POINTS AND WIN BY AT LEAST TWO POINTS.

VOLLEYBALL PROS

Girls who love and **excel** at indoor volleyball can play the sport in college. In 2021, a **professional** indoor volleyball **league** for women began play in the United States. It's called Athletes Unlimited. There are also professional leagues in other countries.

WOMEN'S INDOOR VOLLEYBALL WORLD CUP, 2018 ISTANBUL, TURKEY

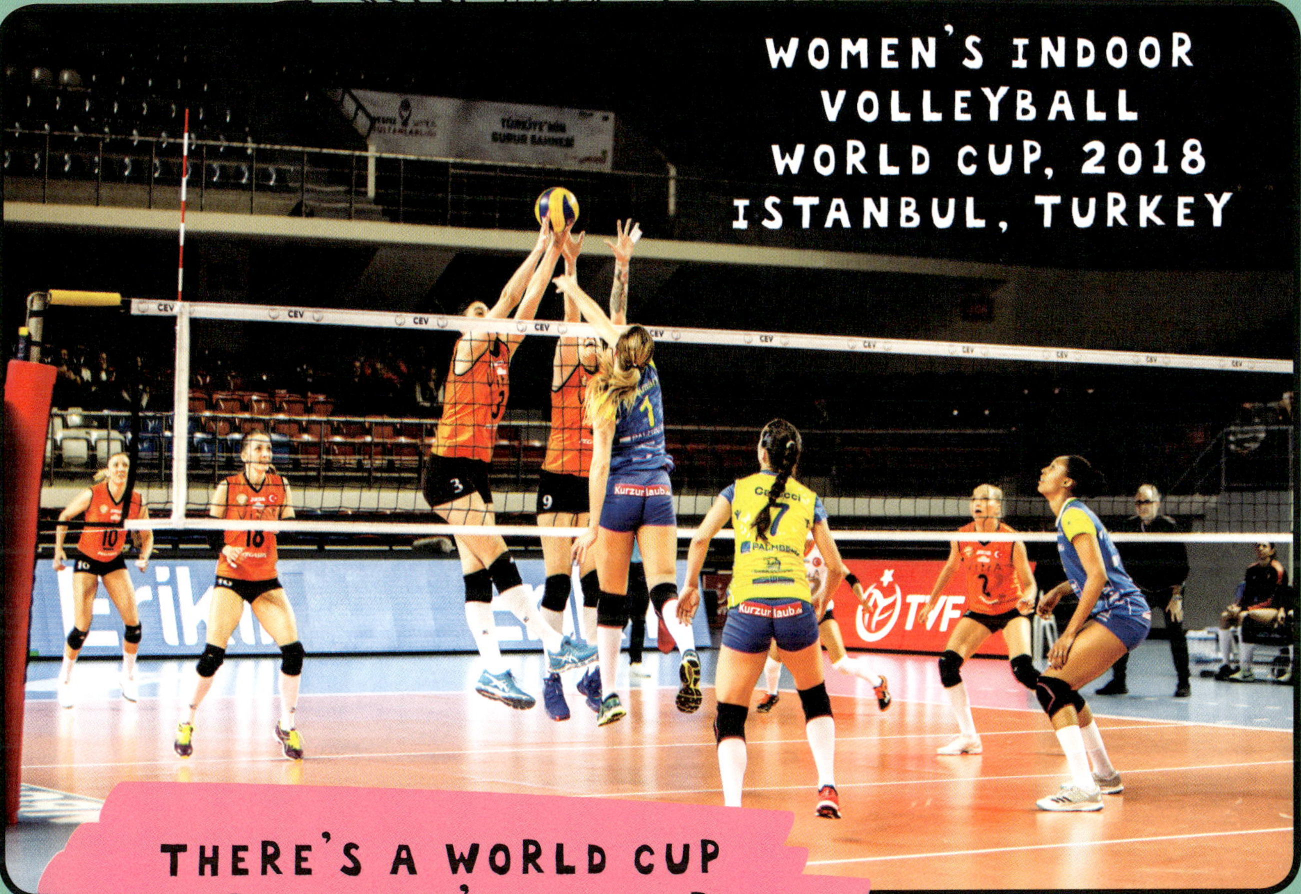

THERE'S A WORLD CUP FOR WOMEN'S INDOOR VOLLEYBALL TOO!

OLYMPIC DREAMS

Indoor volleyball became an Olympic sport for both men and women at the 1964 Summer Olympics. In 2021, the U.S. women's indoor volleyball national team won a gold **medal** at the Summer Olympics in Tokyo, Japan!

2021 USA VOLLEYBALL'S WOMEN'S NATIONAL TEAM

TEAM USA BEAT BRAZIL TO WIN GOLD IN 2021.

Words to Know

championship A contest to find out who's the best player or team in a sport.

clockwise The direction that the hands of a clock move when you look at it from the front.

commit To do something—often something that is wrong.

excel To be or do better than others.

fault Any playing action that goes against the rules.

league A group of teams that play the same sport and compete against each other.

medal A flat, small piece of metal with art or words that's used as an honor or reward.

professional Having to do with a job someone does for a living.

serve To throw a ball into the air and hit it over a net to start play in a volleyball game.

FOR MORE INFORMATION

Books

Downs, Kieran. *Volleyball*. Minneapolis, MN: Bellwether Media, Inc., 2021.

Gitlin, Marty. *Olympic Volleyball Legends*. Mankato, MN: Bolt is published by Black Rabbit Books, 2021.

Websites

Rules of Volleyball
usavolleyball.org/play/rules-of-volleyball/
Discover all the different rules of volleyball and the many kinds that are out there.

Women's National Team
usavolleyball.org/womens-national-team/
Follow USA Volleyball's Women's National Team on their website.

Publisher's note to educators and parents: Our editors have carefully reviewed these websites to ensure that they are suitable for students. Many websites change frequently, however, and we cannot guarantee that a site's future contents will continue to meet our high standards of quality and educational value. Be advised that students should be closely supervised whenever they access the internet.

INDEX

Athlete's Unlimited, 18
beach/outdoor volleyball, 8
championship, 7
college, 18
court, 8, 12
indoor volleyball, 8, 9, 10, 14
match, 11, 16
Morgan, William G., 6
moving positions, 15
net, 6, 10, 12
Olympics, 20
professional leagues, 18
serve, 12, 14
set, 11, 16
teamwork, 4
U.S. Women's National Team, 20
Women's Indoor Volleyball World Cup, 19